W9-CUD-146

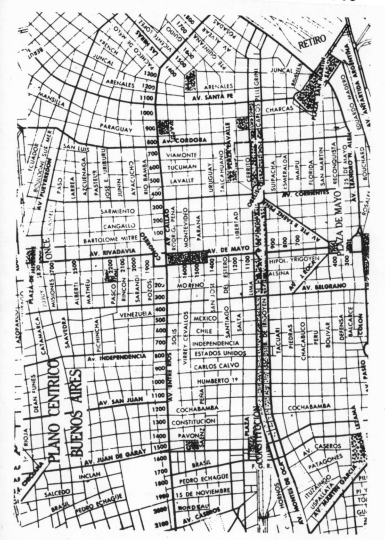

Tartagal
San Ramón de la Nva. Orán
San Salvador de Jujuy
Salta
Formosa Gral.
Pt. Iguazú
Pres. R. Saenz Peña
Charato
San Martín
Resitencia
El Dorado
San Miguel de Tucumán
Río Hondo
V. Angela
Corrientes
Posadas
Santiago del Estero
San del V. de Catamar.
La Rioja
Curuzu Cuatiá
P. de los Libres
Mte. Caseros
San Juan
Córdoba
Santa Fe
V. Dolores
Concordia
Paraná
Mendoza
San Luis
Rosario
Río Cuarto
Gualeguaychú
San Rafael
Gral. Pico
Gualeguay
I.M. García
Buenos Aires
Santa Rosa
Azul
Tandil
Cnel. Suarez
Neuquen
Tres Arroyos
Bahía Blanca
Mar del Plata
Necochea
San Antonio Oeste
C. de Patagones
Viedma
San C. de Bariloche
Esquel
Trelew

OCEANO PACIFICO

OCEANO ATLANTICO

Sarmiento
Comodoro Rivadavia
P. Moreno
Pt. Deseado
Gdor. Gregores
San Julián
Calafate
Santa Cruz
Río Turbio
Río Gallegos

Islas Malvinas (Arg.)
Pto. Stanley

Río Grande
Ushuaia

▲ Aeropuertos Internacionales
● Cludades con servicios de aeronavegación

Mapa de la República Argentina. Lineas aérea

BUENOS AIRES
YOUR POCKET GUIDE
EVA L. KANTOR
1978


Translated and adapted
from original:
  "Pequeña Guía Turística de
  la Ciudad de Buenos Aires"
  Alberto C. Di Pietro


**Cover page, Photography
and diagram: Susana Malatrasi**


EDITORIAL DIAGRAF

SALTA 389  37-4198

**AÑO 1978**

# PREFACE

From the very moment you began to plan your trip you had entered the fantastic land of tourism.

As long as it is a unit, you are allowed to be an active partner of this human being recreational laboratory. Actually, there is no simple formula to define this captivating activity but anyhow we are all engaged in this phenomenon.

Tourism is correlated with different scientific disciplines. It covers an ample range, specially sociology, economy, culture, religion, sports, etc. But the first aim is the contribution to a better understanding among people, and of course from this connection it results such a profitable approach that no other phenomena has succeeded to achieve before. By means of such a peculiar methodology, the touristic activity develops positive links.

In the past you were a stranger, now, after stepping on our city, we are sharing many subjects. Therefore it is possible to create a whole, full of reciprocal respect and human warmth, with imperishable ties.

To summarize, it is useless to come to definitions, when the real goal is to know each other in amicable terms, as passengers we are of the living-tour in our planet.

# STARTING POINT

**DEAR READER:**

This pocket guide of the city of Buenos Aires has been written specially for you.

It is a pleasure to welcome you together with the wish of a happy stay. All necessary and useful information you could need is offered, as far as possible, throughout its contents.

The main objetives are:

To offer a knowledge of the city in such a way you would be in condition to acquire an integrated view of said and as a result, to keep it as a remembrance.

To facilitate a direct access to the most important national products.

To awaken your participation on the ample range of activities this cosmopolitan city possesses.

To "discover" Buenos Aires is always a fascination. This guide pledges you to live together such a wonderful experience.

# BUENOS AIRES CITY

*May Square*

The city of Buenos Aires, on the right bank of RIO DE LA PLATA (River Plate) was founded for the first time in 1536, by the Spanish conqueror Don Pedro de Mendoza. But only after 1580, another conqueror Don Juan de Garay, placed it where May Square is found nowadays.

The natural development of the modern metropolis enlarged its original center up to its present limits, which covers 190 square kilometers. This town presents a main characteristic: the easy detection of its borders. On the northeast the tremendous "Río de la Plata"; running from north to south, the "AVENIDA GENERAL PAZ" fixes its western border, at the same time dividing the capital city and the province of Buenos Aires. On the south, the natural limit with the same province is pointed out by the "RIACHUELO".

The population of the city itself plus the one of the urban surroundings called "GRAN BUENOS AIRES" amounts to about eight million inhabitants. For this reason it is the largest Spanish speaking city all over the world.

Buenos Aires has a varied net of transportation means: "AEROPARQUE JORGE NEWBERY" (Jorge Newbery Airport) in the city itself, in front of the river bank. The "AEROPUERTO INTERNACIONAL DE EZEIZA" (International Ezeiza Airport) linked to the capital by means of an important super highway. Furthermore there is the huge Buenos Aires harbour, where oversealiners and miscellaneous vessels arrive on a daily schedule. Four railway terminal stations which connect with neighbouring countries; they are: Retiro, Constitución, Once and Federico Lacroze. It also offers the tourists a great variety of bus lines, joining the farthest areas of the inland as well as the boundary countries; finally, five urban subway lines interconnect the main quarters of the city.

Although the structure of itts buildings and the demographic development has a defined Spanish and Italian origin, the large number of immigrants that arrived to its coasts for over a century up to now, from all parts of the world, contributed to its

*Retiro – Panoramic view*

improvement and granted this town a peculiar cosmopolitan style. This may be easily noticed by tourists and visitors, thus justifying the assertion that you will find the "crucible of nationalities".

Though the general context offers a european appearance, that is to say a "migratory center", it shows unmistakable Argentine features of a strong personality, nourished by deep national historical roots.

At first sight Buenos Aires puzzles the tourists through the great variety of activities it offers everywhere. Just walking along its streets, infers a peculiar architectonic style, resulting from the intense commercial and industrial haste.

This characteristic of the city is clearly shown by means of the thoughtful and harmonic design of downtown area, embellished fro and through by lots of squares, parks, gardens, statues and artistic monuments of magnificent beauty.

Night entertainments offer a highlight variety of attractions: theatres, with first rate national and international casts on stage; the so-called "revista-show" (show parades) in a bright and colourful scenography; café-concerts (kind of vaudeville performance) of sparkling humour; night clubs, where night after night famous artists entertain the guests; sophisticated cosy boites, a great number of cinemas, with worldwide simultaneous hit premieres.

Argentine grade "A" meat suggests restaurants as other attractive places where to be acquainted with its national way of life. Native grills (including barbecues - asados) where folk specialties may please the most deserving gourmet, contend with finest international cooking, served in first class restaurants.

Sports events are known all over the world, attracting an enthusiastic crowd of fans, on account of the high proficiency and technical level attained both in domestic and world games and championships.

The native of Buenos Aires is called "porteño" due to the fact that the city grows around the important port. The "porteño" goes hand in hand with the "lunfardo", popular jargon spoken in this city and in the whole country, mixture of a kind

*Old lighters — Riachuelo*

of slang words. This language, common to all social levels, has a particular affective and sociological inference.

The porteño's fellow partner is the "tango", popular music of the Argentines, strongly tightened to their feelings and longings. Such a peculiar blending attracted the attention of poets, writers, musicians and artists, and all of them felt the need to express each one, in their own viewpoint and sensibility, stressing the particularities of this special way of being.

Jorge Luis Borges, Homero Manzi, Enrique Santos Discépolo, Evaristo Carriego, Carlos Gardel, Julio Cortázar, Francisco Canaro, Aníbal Troilo, Astor Piazzola, Raúl Soldi, Juan Carlos Castagnino, Antonio Berni, among other famous personalities impressed fundamental aspects of these interwoven deeds in their masterpieces.

The "porteño" is diligent, good-natured, and above all noble-minded. To ask freely for his help is particularly easy, beacause he is always ready to grant a favor or "hacer una gauchada" as the Argentine-like jargon goes.

11

## Plaza Libertador General San Martín (San Martín Square)

Located within Santa Fe Avenue, Maipú Street, Leandro N. Alem Avenue and Florida Street, this wonderful slope has on its western top side, the monument to General José de San Martín, giving it his name. This statue has been there since February 25th, 1878, centenary of the Liberator's birth.

*Monument – General José de San Martín.*

## Florida

It is captivating at first glance. People walking inceasingly to and fro San Martín square up to Rivadavia street shape it with an unusual dynamism. It is the only pedestrian street of Buenos Aires. Those who are working or just going for a walk, feel pleased to step along this street embellished with plants and flowerpots. Multicolored bookstalls offer newpapers, magazines and posters, from the country and abroad, reminding pictures of an impressionistic style.

Shopping in this street ressembles a feast. Department stores, boutiques, tailor's, shoemaker's, book shops, and a lot of commercial promenades offer all kind of goods and articles.

Important galleries of art, with occasional and permanent exhibitions enhance the interest that Argentine people show for fine arts.

All along you find overcrowded hotels, banks, exchange agencies, restaurants and coffe-houses, tearooms, snack bars. People reading and discussing over local and international news,

*Florida Street — Let's go shopping*

announced by a centenary morning paper, give this street a special brand.

That is why thousands of "porteños", walking through Florida street, feel proud of it.

## Córdoba Avenue

Bordered by a kind of matching buildings, it has a dense automotive traffic. All types of shops, tourism agencies, shipping and air companies, exchange agencies, hotels, snack bars and restaurants are located here.

## Lavalle

Because the part within the limits of Florida and 9 de Julio Avenue is full of cinemas, it is known as "la calle de los cines" (street of cinemas).

Restaurants and "pizzerías" are habitually crowded by visitors of this singular street.

## Corrientes Avenue

This deeply rooted "porteña" avenue is visited on, day and night, by all sorts of people.

From Eduardo Madero avenue on, where the Luna Park Stadium is located, up to Callao avenue, there are theatres, cinemas, restaurants, and different entertainment places. All those wishing to acquire the last news about books and records, will find them among a variety of shops.

After Callao and up to Pueyrredón avenue, a picturesque commercial center is settled, full of shops with all sorts of goods and articles, on a peculiar display. Corrientes avenue as well as its surroundings have the wholesale and retail active commerce of the city. "Once" (name of the quarter) owns

14

clothes, cloth, furs, wool and leather articles, among other possibilities to be bought, of full consuming and supply all year round.

### Plaza de Mayo (May Square)

It is surrounded by Rivadavia avenue, Bolívar street, Hipólito Irigoyen and Balcarce street. The May Pyramid, symbol of the historical and revolutionary movement of 1810 is on its center.

On east there stands the Government House called "Casa Rosada" (Pink House) place of the headquarters of Executive Power. The Cabildo, a national monument, pure image of Argentine history, looks on at the huge "Río de la Plata".

*Centennary gumtrees – Our historical square*

The Metropolitan Cathedral, having on its right part the mausoleum with the remains of General José de San Martín, is towards northeast. Surrounding this historical square there are public buildings like: Municipality of the city of Buenos Aires, Social Welfare Ministry, Banco de la Nación Argentina, etc.

## May Avenue

It begins exactly in May Square and pointing from this point we find the most ancient porteño newspaper. From its first blocks Spanish style buildings are visited by citizens of the same nationality. A nostalgic air of Madrid is given by the peculiar meetings, in typical coffe-houses and tearooms, with tables and chairs on the paths. Old hotels, cinemas, and theatres, where plays of hispanic origin are performed, give all of them a kind of special atmosphere.

*May Avenue (Madrid in Buenos Aires)*

## Rivadavia Avenue

This avenue of Buenos Aires accompanies the sun day after day. Although it begins on east, it still continues being porteña towards west, until it reaches Avenida General Paz. Once beyond it and before entering Argentine pampa, following Domingo Faustino Sarmiento railway line stops (among beautiful sites of "Gran Buenos Aires") it continues as national route N° 7, formerly called "camino real" (royal road).

The most remarkable characteristics of this avenue lays upon the fact that it divides the city into two different parts.

*Rivadavia Avenue*
*(Art Noveau)*

Transversal streets begin there, taking their number and names towards south and north.

This avenue runs through the city, with a singular and characteristic seal: the impressing constant changes of the peculiar features the quarters it goes through offer.

Being narrow at first, within downtown area, when it reaches "Plaza Congreso" (Congreso Square) — passing through the place fixed as the starting point, 0 km, for all national routes, it takes the traditional forms of all big avenues.

Plaza Once (Once Square) is the convergence of an unaccountable number of bus lines, a railway station, and the intense commercial movement of the zone. Rapid traffic goes along, and this continues up to "Caballito" quarter (line "A" subway terminal, called "Primera Junta").

A variety of architectonic styles built along Rivadavia avenue shows the city wide enlargement. The arrogance of "Flores" quarter, the peacefulness of "La Floresta" quarter, and the quietness of "Villa Luro", are strictly opposed to the puissant activity displayed in "Liniers", a starting point towards the small but populous cities of Gran Buenos Aires.

## 9 de Julio Avenue

This wide avenue runs along the city from north to south, from farther than Santa Fe avenue, up to Plaza Constitución. Different kinds of skyscrapers could be seen when passing this wonderful tracksweep, as well as small and woody squares, bearing the names of Argentine provinces. Nice fountains and beautiful jacarandaes with light blue, violet and yellow flowers, garnish this avenue, thus suggesting a formidable view.

In the intersection of 9 de Julio avenue with Corrientes, there stands the "Plaza de la República". The Obelisk, built in 1936, commemorating the 400 years of the foundation of the city is on its center. This monument is the one that identifies the porteño himself with his metropolis. Huge advertising posters light up the city night with sparkling colours.

*Small square*

*Colon Theatre*

When reaching Tucumán street, on this same avenue, the impossing building of Teatro Colón (Colón Theatre) of original style and conception appears. Inaugurated on May 25th 1908, it is the prized aim for famous artists of classic music, dance and international lyrics.

## Plaza Congreso (Congreso Square)

Its surroundings are Rivadavia avenue, Entre Ríos Avenue, Hipólito Irigoyen and Luis Sáenz Peña street.

This wide square is ornamented by the attractive monument "A los dos Congresos" and by the sculptural masterpieces of high aesthetic value. The reproduction of "El Pensador" by Augusto Rodin, is the oustanding one.

On Entre Ríos avenue the big building of the national Congress raises (site of the Legislative Power) an impossing architectonic structure which overlooks the square. It has an equilibrium of classic and greco-roman elements.

*The Congress*

## Callao Avenue

This is one of the most significant downtown avenues. On its beginning stands a traditional and almost centennial tearoom, meeting place for important public men as well as for old patrician Argentine families.

Hotels, restaurants, snack bars and all kinds of shops are constantly visited by people eager of shopping.

Crossing Santa Fe avenue and up to Libertador avenue it acquires a special prestige, given by luxurious residences, splendid hotels and sophisticated shops.

## Santa Fe Avenue

It calls your attention because refined young and gay people daily visit this avenue. It appears to be a fixed appointment for all those eager to walk and to watch up to date fashion costumes.

Due to its stylish promenades, modern airlines companies premises, comfortable hotels and nice public and private buildings, the name of "la gran vía del norte" (the great northern avenue) had been granted to it.

A great number of shops are seen in an endless line, reflecting a special good taste.

Even though the principal center is between San Martín square and Callao avenue, variety of this active commercial life is not disminished up to Palermo.

## Alvear Avenue

French style residences clear up the way to "Basílica Menor de Nuestra Señora del Pilar" (Pilar church) and its centennial gum-trees. This classic perspective is enriched by the sophisticated splendour of galleries and shops.

People wishing to find out exclusive designs will be rewarded in their search because creativity plays the first role in this area.

Be sure your eyes will have a charming pleasure when walking along this avenue.

## Libertador Avenue

The rectilineal design of this avenue, after having gone along one side of Retiro Station, goes across the green squares of la Recoleta quarter, under the shadows of its gum-trees, leading afterwards right towards the northern part of the city, parallel to Río de la Plata.

Embassies, consulates, important museums and the most modern buildings complete its decoration, showing always gay, day and night.

It runs through Palermo, to finish its way within the capital in Núñez quarter, where the most populated clubs of the metropolis are lined up.

*A sight – Monument "Magna Chartra and the Four Argentine Regions"*

# A WALK ALONG THE QUARTERS

## Plaza San Martín y Retiro

A splendid panoramic view is offered by a group of green squares and the characteristic buildings of barrio Retiro. San Martín square with a surface of 27730 square meters keeps a privileged place over the slope.

Through history, as long as years had gone by, it changed into different names. It is assumed that on the end of XVII siecle, there was the "Ermita de San Sebastián" (Hermitage), a lot devoted to monks spiritual abstraction. Due to this fact it had been given the name of "El Retiro" which still remains the same for the area of Córdoba avenue, Leandro N. Alem avenue, Libertador avenue and Esmeralda street.

*"La Duda" – Sculpture of the square*

Afterwards it was a black slaves market of the English Royal Company, and then a bull-fight square. In 1807 it took the name of "Campo de la Gloria" as a remembrance for those who had fought against English invasions, but in 1823 it was called

25

"Campo de Marte" (Marte Campus) because an important head-quarter was built on Arenales street.

The silhouette of the monumnet of Libertador General San Martín is seen over the ample lawn. Inaugurated in July 13th 1862, it was assigned the definite name of "Plaza San Martín" (San Martín square) in 1878, centenary of the hero's birth.

A site full of people and enriched with beauty, at the same time keeps the constant homages before the maximum hero of American independence.

Within this area there appear: the Plaza Hotel, first in style and size, opened in July, 1909; the Kavanagh building, inaugurated in 1936, a remembrance of the architectonic fashion of

*Seaver Path — Urbanistic curiosity*

*A sight – Monument
– General San Martín*

such an epoch. In Maipú street the "Círculo Militar or Palacio
Paz" stands since 1902, reminding the part of the Louvre
belonging to the XVII siecle. Palacio San Martín, seat of the
Ministry of Public Affairs, is on Arenales street; while in San
Martín 1039 *it* is the "Basílica del Santísimo Sacramento", 1908,
sacred on July 1916. The Buenos Aires Sheraton Hotel, inaugurated in 1972, stands by.

Among the small squares called: Juvenilia, Salvador María
del Carril, Britania and Canadá, the monuments play together
with the harmonious distribution of botanical species. A popular
tower "Torre de los Ingleses" bestowed in 1916 by the British
community, marks in four big clocks time passing, for hurried
porteños, all along Retiro station.

*Retiro Station – English Tower*

This terminal station is the starting point of different railway lines, joining farthest areas of the republic as well as boundary countries.

**Plaza de Mayo y Catedral al Sur (May Square and southern Cathedral quarter)**

A light constant fluttering of pigeons along it, recall the clamor for independencia and freedom in May 25th, 1910.

When Garay settled in 1580 the city of Buenos Aires for the second time, this site was taken for the main square. Change of

*May Pyramid —*
*Historical place*

epochs and needs have produced important modifications upon it. Since 1942 it has been declared historical place.

The May Pyramid is a clear testimony of Argentine spirit since May 25th, 1811. The statue of Liberty over its top, the date of independence with a rising sun on its center, and the national emblem on its base, play a suitable role.

The Government House has an imposing entrance gate, pilasters with complex capitals, lots of columns and windows, adorned mouldings and slate roofs, all pertaining the electic style.

A fight between white and red political parties was the origin, in the past siecle, of the decision to paint with a pink colour this building showing an attempt to unify politic passions of such an epoch. From then on, it was called "Casa Rosada" (Pink House).

*Government House – National Executive Power site*

"El Cabildo" the parliament of the colonical time (official place for important meetings), was begun to be built in 1608; nowadays it is a historical museum. The building we can see today was designed by Andrés Blanqui in 1725; when May avenue and Diagonal Julio A. Roca were opened, three arches of each side disappeared. It integrates the unit of museums of the city of Buenos Aires, because of its important pictorial art collections, religious and popular, rich furniture, weapons, ensigns and flags, all belonging to colonial epochs. You are strongly recommended to visit it.

The metropolitan cathedral has a kind of harmonic facade with the votive lamp as an homage to General San Martín and the unknown soldier of our independencia, together with twelve solid columns representing the apostles and a triangular frontispiece, keeping a biblical raised work. The last structure of this building had been done by architect Antonio Masella in 1791.

From the big central nave it is possible to watch the solemnity of its interior, which is accompanied by the renaissance italian styled decoration, performed by painter Francisco Parisi.

*Cabildo – (The Parliament of colonial time).*

*Metropolitan Cathedral – Facade*

Alsina and Defensa is a typical porteño corner, whereas historical masterpieces buildings are combined. In 1754 San Francisco church was built, with a peculiar characteristic: a single nave about 90 meters in length. At the back of the high altar it is the extraordinary tapestry, designed by painter Horacio Butler, and done in this country.

*San Francisco Church*
*— Towers*

Old San Roque Chapel, built in 1751, keeps inside carved wooden and polychromed images of the XVIII siecle. This chapel possesses the greatest subterranean cementery belonging to old Buenos Aires.

"La Estrella", old pharmacy, keeps the characteristics of the epoch wholly untouched, with rich decorating allegories. On its first floor, with an entrance through Alsina street, the museum of the city is located.

The four peaceful white marble statues representing: Navigation, Industry, Astronomy and Geography, had been the complementing ornament of the May Pyramid in the past century.

The facade of San Ignacio Church comes off in Alsina and Bolívar since 1722. Close to it is the "Colegio Nacional de Buenos Aires" (Secondary School) educational place of prestige, where distinguished Argentine men have studied; it was founded by Viceroy Vertiz in 1783.

Juan B. Ambrosetti had installed in Moreno 350 the Ethnographic Museum (1904) and it still continues as such. The ample collection of archaeological pieces of native and foreign cultures as well as a large library, is permanently consulted by specialists, as a treasure of the national patrimony.

The ancestral manor house that Santo Domingo Church has in Belgrano and Defensa Street, is a national historical monument since 1942. It is linked to the Argentine soul by affective ties,

*Santo Domingo Church – A sight*

33

and it is the guardian of the mausoleum of Manuel Belgrano, the creator of the national flag.

Different historical events which have happened near it, make the visit to this church be one of special devotion.

The marks left by the bullets shot during the English Invasion could be seen on top of the left tower. When entering the church its imposing organ placed on its high altar stands out. Four English Flags obtained during the invasion and two argentine given by Belgrano, are placed at the back of the left nave. But not everything is historical here, boites, restaurants and theatres are the adequate complement to make an unforgettable ride out of this.

### San Telmo

Paved streets of narrow paths, corners without octaves, antique colonial mansions of Italian and Spanish influence, strong and waving grates, tiles with grass, and strong doors with window panes, bring back suggesting scenes of the past.

*Carlos Calvo and Balcarce — A traditional place*

*Parque Lezama – Fountain and amphitheatre*

Although placed in the southern corner of the city, it is one of the smallest and most ancient quarter of it. About seventy blocks are included in this zone, limited by Paseo Colón and Martín García avenues, and Chacabuco and Chile streets.

It was an active urban center, constantly busy with carts carrying merchandises from far away places of the country to "Altos de San Pedro" nowadays Dorrego square, up to 1870, when an epidemy of "fiebre amarilla" (yellow fever) compelled the inhabitants to transfer their shops to the northern part of Plaza de Mayo.

In San Telmo the metropolis had grown: it was a scenery of historical events; it gave birth to intellectuals; shelter for religious congregations and charming place for pilgrims. Tender remembrances of the past are kept here.

A frontal ravine washed by the waters of the Río de la Plata attracted Don Pedro de Mendoza who chose such a spot to establish the old city of Buenos Aires in 1536. An attractive monument in Defensa Street and Brasil shows this historical event.

*Parque Lezama – A typical path*

The urbanistic development separated the ravine from its friendly river. At present it is bordered by noisy avenues, showing a proud beauty to the daily growing city.

Time went on and granted it different owners: Don Gregorio Lezama, the last one, attached to the place, enriched the natural beauty of the spot with exotic plants, peaceful paths, sunny paths, and picturesque fountains. Beloved Lezama square has turned to be a public walk. Children laughter, song of birds and the quiet rest of old people go together in it.

There is a manorial house with italic influence, dating 1897, which has been appointed national museum. Its doors open to

Defensa Street and treasures of high value are sheltered in thirty rooms.

*National Historical Museum*

Traditional Dorrego square, in Humberto I and Defensa Street, is the second most ancient square of the city, being Plaza de Mayo the first one. On Sundays, from early morning up to sunset, it has an peculiar fair of antiquities. Artisans offer the possibility to acquire strange, may be needless, but always beautiful things.

The dynamic equilibrium of the size, of space and the strong inner force which flow from each one of the beautiful figures of the statue "Canto al Trabajo" (Song to Work) call the attention

*A sight – "Song to work" (Rogelio Yrurtia)*

of those walking by Olazábal square, in Paseo Colón Avenue and Independence Avenue. This splendid sculptoric work is a masterpiece of the famous argentine artist Rogelio Yrurtia, dating 1911.

San Telmo has three churches belonging each one to different religions: San Pedro González Telmo, in Humberto I 340—Nuestra Señora de Belén is worshipped there. It is a historical monument since 1942, with an eminent baroque facade, richly ornamented. In Brasil 315, the "Catedral Ortodoxa Rusa de la Santísima Trinidad" (Russian Orthodox Cathedral) shows its five

*San Pedro González
Telmo Church*

domes and a wonderful interior, typical characteristics of the byzantine russian style. The Danish church, of sober nordic lines stands in Carlos Calvo 260. It was inaugurated in 1931 and belongs to the Lutheran religion.

An intrincated labyrinth of mysterious tunnels, earnestly keeps veiled unknown secrets, while the night in San Telmo is generous to visitors. Aristocratic restaurants, cafe concerts and theatres, old bars and "tanguerías" are joined in this small "republic".

Close to San Telmo, in Independencia 1799, stands the "House of Spiritual Practice". Its wide walls, chapels, rooms for meditation, the yards and inner galleries, keep works of religious imagery and a buystanding furniture. Although it was finished in 1799, it still continues being the purest sample of colonial architectonic style.

*Russian Orthodox Cathedral "Santísima Trinidad"*

## La Boca

A geometrical structure of iron and cement on the side of the river, an intense cromatic vibration covering the ondulated texture of the houses, old lighters which dream with unforgotten trips and an expectant mast, give a welcome to "La Boca" quarter.

40

A little river and a narrow curve of the outlet, had watched the birth of the only port of Buenos Aires, long before the XVIII century. The "Riachuelo" and "La vuelta de Roca" gave the original name to this place: "La Boca del Riachuelo".

*A view – Riachuelo and Nicolás Avellaneda Bridge*

Barracks, salting-places, some "pulperías" (retail groceries) and some humble houses, marked the bank of the river, when it was still known as "Pueblo de la Boca" (quarter). Its limits enlarged in August 26th 1870, and it was officially named "Barrio de la Boca".

With the arrival of the ship "Italia", the first transatlantic with high draft, bringing genoese inmigrants, its local activity started to grow. The need to communicate themselves gave as a result that the genoese dialect introduced linguistic idioms into the "porteño" speech, to such an extent that it became quickly a part of popular language. Some words and idioms are still found in the "lunfardo" (popular speech), with peculiar characteristics, always changing.

*"Vuelta de Rocha"*
*– Boca*

In the curious square of "La vuelta de Rocha", a mast, lines, sheaves, anchor, ladders, give their homage from June 20th 1945 onwards, to all those sailors who arrived here. The statue of Admiral Guillermo Brown remembers that brave hero of the sea, who, with love and talent built there the ships which were used during the battles of our independence.

A dusty little road (a little river in the past) inspired in 1926 the great musician Juan de Dios Filiberto to create the tango "Caminito".

Thirty years later, the untiring argentine painter Benito Quinquela Martín, who had fallen in love with that place, wanted to offer the musical masterpiece a visual background. He organi-

*Caminito Street*

zed and ornamented with his talent this picturesque place, which he enriched with strong colours of his palette, motivating other artists to contribute to adorn it.

The School Museum Pedro de Mendoza, placed in Pedro de Mendoza 1835, and inaugurated in 1936, owns its creation to the worthy idea of Benito Quinquela Martín, who bestowed the lot of the National Council of Education.

In the first floors a pilot kindergarden and a primary school are found, decorated with masterpieces of this "boquense" artist. Once through the door there appear carved works of polychromatic wood, product of skillful artists; they are kept in the room "Mascarones de Proa" (shields of bow) which clearly demonstrate the sea origin of "La Boca". The rest of the rooms have 700 paintings, and two are the conditions to accept works to be placed there, and very unusual ones: they must belong to Argentine artists and must represent the so called figurative art. Fernando Fader, Ernesto de la Cárcova, Eduardo Sívori, Fortunato de la Cámera, Lino E. Spilimbergo, Antonio Alice, Antonio

Berni, Raúl Soldi, Enrique Policastro and others complete the collection. In the ample terraces, where the sculptures make a sole piece with space, the noble and rhythmic works of artists are gathered: Rogelio Yrurtia, Alberto Lagos, Pedro Zonza Briano, Luis Falcini, Agustín Riganelli, Luis Perlotti, etc. Surrounded by a very clear atmosphere, the study Museum Benito Quinquela Martín describes a vision of the port environment faithfully reflected through his pictorial themes.

*Pedro de Mendoza Museum — Terraces*

The Ribera theatre, the "Lactarium" (nursing room) and the children's odontologic Institute, are other works which remark the prolific task performed by this artist.

The inhabitants of "La Boca" unify their sport passion gathering around the colours of the club they love: Boca Juñiors Club, which has its stadium in Brandsen and Del Valle Iberlucea streets, known with the affective name of "La Bombonera".

When the night comes, walking along Necochea street, nobody can escape the temptation to go into one of the nice "cantinas", to enjoy the familiarity of the "boquense" attention.

*A balcony – Boca*

## Recoleta

This quarter has taken its name from the Convent of the Recolects Monks, built in 1716. The harmonious perfection and the exact place of the elements which compose it, are the main causes of its elegance.

The body formed by the Art Museum, the Faculty of Law and the National Rooms for Exhibition offers a particular tone inside the attractive natural landscape of this part of Recoleta.

*Faculty of Law and Social Sciences*

The National Museum of Art, created by decree of the Executive Power in 1895, occupies since 1931, the building of Libertador Avenue N° 1473.

Carlos Morel, Prilidiano Pueyrredón, Fernando Fader, Eduardo Sívori, Carlos de la Cárcova, Martín Malharro, Emilio Petorutti, Pablo Curatela, are among a group, some of the artists who gave their talent as an important contribution to argentine fine art. Their works and those belonging to foreign ones, which amount to 8.000 pieces, form the patrimony of the museum. The Public Library, specialized in fine arts, inside this same museum, has a collection of 30.000 books.

In 1960, when the sesquicentennial of Mayo Revolution was celebrated, an attached lodge was built, where important periodic expositions take place.

In Posadas 1725, the National Rooms for Exhibitions are placed, which are appointed to hold periodic exhibitions of arts and which attract the interest of public. This place in sentimentally linked to the "tango", since from the beginnning

*"Centauro Herido" – Sculpture (Antoine Boudelle)*

of the century (called "Palais de Glace") gathered the first admirers of the popular "porteña" music it Perhaps a magnetism of its own had imposed this building to be the first one about twenty years ago, where the first images of argentine T.V. were taken from.

The small square placed at the end of Posadas Street enlarges itself showing the outstanding sculptural work made by Antoine Bourdelle, dedicated to General Carlos M. de Alvear. The rigorous geometric lines which govern the works of this skilfull French author, determine this to be one of the most perfect equestrian statues of the world. Four beautiful figures surround this monument, symbolizing Victory, Liberty, Strength and Eloquence.

47

This work was done in Paris and was lately transported to Buenos Aires, where it was inaugurated by the end of 1926.

*"Heracles" — Sculpture (Antonio Bourdelle)*

On Presidente Figueroa Alcorta Avenue 2363, the Faculty of Law and Social Sciences shows its neo-classic facade of sober lines, which seems to countercheck with the constant movement of thousands of young people which this building receives year after year.

For those who want to enjoy entertaiment, it is possible to find the "Ital Park" as the exact place where go. It is placed in the junction of Libertador Avenue and Callao Street, and because of its extension it is the biggest in South America. Ghost trains, original merry-go-round, electric cars, round the world games, and a lot of other entertaintment, which both kids and grown ups enjoy.

The international status of its shops, hoteles, tea rooms, restaurants and boites constitute the exquisite personality of this quarter.

*"Basílica" – Nuestra Señora del Pilar – Church of colonnial art*

The historical elements which show the colonnial past of the city, find in "The Basilica de Nuestra Señora del Pilar" (Pilar Church) the best example.

A very simple facade, a porch with quarterns and on its left side the only tower of glazed tile cupola allow the shining of the blackmoore with double arch, which makes an end to its right

49

side. The architect, designer of this construction, could see it finished in 1732.

A baroque interior, the highly esteemed lateral altars, the relics and nice imagery work prearrange the spirit of the parishioners who reach the secular high altar.

Since 1942 this "Basilica" is a national historical monument. The "Recoleta cementery" is on its right hand, it was previously known as Northern Churchyard, it was opened in 1822. The "Panteón de los Próceres" (Grandee Mausoleum) composed by the sepulture of several of our patriots is considered National historical monument, and it is under the guard of the state. A statue of Our Redeemer is placed in the middle of it, a masterpiece of Argentine sculptor Pedro de Lozano Briano.

The spiritual unity of this area is given by the Convent of the Franciscan Recollect, which is placed on the left of the Basilica.

In Alvear Square, the craftsmen of Buenos Aires, gather in an original fair, which is opened during the week-ends and on holiday days. Objects of creative artisan work are exhibited and sold there.


**Palermo**

The gay eyes of those who hear the name of Palermo, reflect the pleasure this lighted area inspires.

The small "Italia square" and the monument to José Garibaldi seem to show the starting point towards the countless rides which this frondose square of 200 hectares of extension proposes.

To walk up and down these triflingly nice paths, with lots of statues and fountains, pacify the spirit of those who visit the Botanical Garden. The rational distribution of native and foreign samples of plants, work of landscapist Carlos Thays, was his creation for this fancy porteño garden since 1898.

The already centennial metropolitan zoo "Eduardo Homberg", with many lodges inhabited by animals of the most different species, twisted inner streets, artificial lakes, newstands,

*Palermo Woods – A lake*

theatres and plays, cheer almost two million people visiting it during the year.

The society which gathers the agricultural producers as well as the cattle breeders of the whole country, has big premises for annual expositions. Some industrial fairs of national and foreign products are held in these premises as well, which are visited by lots of people.

The traditional Sarmiento avenue has, when it joins Libertador avenue, the magnificent monument "A la Carta Magna" y "Las cuatro regiones argentinas" (Magna Charta and the four Argentine regions), a masterpiece of Spanish sculptor Agustín Querol. This monument is generally called "De los Españoles" (The Spaniards) because this community bestowed it when the centennial of Mayo revolution was celebrated. It was inaugurated in 1927.

Going along Sarmiento avenue it is located "Parque 3 de Febrero", which gathers different entertaining places. The "Patio Andáluz", the Rosedal, the Japanese garden, the Iran square, the Anfitheatre and also placid lakes.

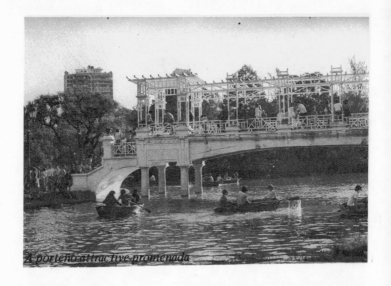
*A porteño attractive promenade*

The K.D.T. circuit for cyclist competitions, the municipal Golf Links, the velodrome, the hippodrome and important clubs, exercise a kind of magnetism for lovers of outside sports.

Spacial structure of the Planetarium "Galileo Galilei" shines on the green grass. Enrique Haus was the architect who designed it, inaugurated in 1966.

The equestrian statue of General Justo José de Urquiza, is the mark for the intersection of Sarmiento avenue and Figueroa Alcorta avenue.

On Libertador avenue N° 1902 it is found an aristrocratic palace, former residence of Matías Errazuriz, Ambassador of Chile in our country, in the first half of the century. It was appointed site of the Decorative Art Museum since 1937, when the Argentine government bought it.

The pictorial collection, the marvellous pieces of the colonial art and the exquisite furniture, enlighten the visitor upon the works done by masters of the speciality.

On the first floor, and as transitory site, it is found the

*Planetarium "Galileo Galilei" – Cultural Center*

Oriental Art Museum, which exhibits highly esteemed treasures of asiatic art.

The area of "Palermo Chico", surrounded by embassies and consulates, has the great pride to hold the Grand Bourg Square, the "Instituto Nacional Sanmartiniano" (San Martín National Institute), residence inaugurated in 1946 and built by architect Julio Salas. It ressembles the house inhabited by General San Martín in France.

## The porteña bank of Río de la Plata (The river)

The confluence of Uruguay and Paraná River in the estuary of "Río de la Plata" forms a gulf of unslated water, 35.000 square km of surface.

Its colour, which is light brown, is the result of all the detritus which the Paraná River brings in the greater part of its way, since the waters brought by the Uruguay river are clean and crystalline.

The so called "Mar Dulce" (sweet sea) by Juan Díaz de Solís

53

*Riverbank masterpiece*

*Sculpture Group — Government House back facade*

*The port of Buenos Aires*

in 1516 changed its name and called it "Río de la Plata" while latter conquerors sailed in against the current of the river, trying to find an exit to the Pacific Ocean. The supposition was that in such a way they would reach the incalculable fortune of the "Sierras de la Plata".

Martín García, its most important island, owns its name due to one of the sailors who accompanied Solís in his expedition. It is Argentina national territory. The warlike events of 1814 which took place near it allowed the most brilliant argentine naval hero to be covered with glory. He was Admiral Guillermo Brown.

At the back of the antique Royal Fortress of Saint Juan Baltasar de Austria, at present government house, the port of Buenos Aires was first created.

Its intense activity, tireless cranes, elevators, big silos of corn, the ululant sirens of the ships which are near the dock divide the two Costanera avenues.

The southern Costanera avenue embellished by the ramblas and picturesque beer-saloons, was the popular municipal bathing place of old times.

The "tucumana" sculptor Dolores Mora de la Vega de Hernández, created in 1903 "Las Nereidas" (The Nereids), sculptures representing Venus birth.

*"Las Nereidas" — Fountain (Argentine sculptor "Lola Mora")*

The bold movement of the naked characters raised then to the most austere criticism. It is nowadays known under the delicate name of "Fuente de Lola Mora" (Lola Mora's fountain).

The sportive city of Boca Juniors Club, harmonious sport site built on lands gained from the river, shows the strength that this populous quarter renders to the club.

The northern Costanera avenue, because of its main situation between "Río de la Plata" and "Bosques de Palermo" (Palermo Woods) is a comfortable way for automotive traffic.

Surrounded by green grass, the tracks of the airport of the city of Buenos Aires "Jorge Newbery" are found, daily welcoming and seeing off a great number of national and foreign planes. The busy life of the airport opposes the calm activity of the fishermen, leaning on breakwater of the Fisher's Club, society that gathers thousands of fans since 1903.

*River Plate – Fishing Club*

The popular beaches are frequented during summer, but the typical "carritos" (a kind of "criollo" restaurante) are visited all year round to taste folk meals by lots of people.

Peacefulness and tranquility which flow from this place, has turned it to be a fixed porteño pleasant custom.

## Belgrano.

Leaving Palermo behind and going north, the puissant Belgrano quarter begins, where ample manorial houses can still be found, being the witness of history, coupling with skyscrapers which show its constant development. The area of woods, which in the XVI century was called "Montes Grandes" got its characteristic of quarter by means of an idea of President Bernardino Rivadavia, and in 1855 it was founded a city with the name of General Manuel Belgrano. In the second part of the last century it shelterd in equal proportions Argentine and foreign inhabitants who imbued ouilding dynamism of special characteristics.

*Mariscal Sucre Square — Buildings*

Greens of the waving banks of Plaza Mariscal José Antonio Sucre (Square) play peace against constant and active local movement. The little paths of old machined bricks lead to the traditional Watch-tower, which accompanied by a little sprout of the Pine of San Lorenzo bestowed on May 25th 1932, make lifelong remembrance of General José de San Martín.

The magnificient blue gum-tree which is five hundred years old offers shadow to all those who go there to play chess games in specially arranged tables. A round summer-house and its curious poligonal roof which was originally used to listen to Municipal bands —of strong root in porteño life— is nowadays transformed into a place where the craftsmen organize their fairs during the weed ends.

*Famous Sculpture (Old "Casa del Angel")*

59

On the stony Echeverría Street and 11 de Septiembre corner, surrounded by a busy traffic, there is a beautiful statue of General Manuel Belgrano which perpetuates his memory. A tilt with number 26 written on it in 11 de Septiembre street, marks the manorial house where Valentín Alsina lived, Argentine politician and founder of this quarter.

The architectonic lines of French influence, characteristic of XVIII century, are shown in the residence of politician Juan Delcasse which was used as a field for "affairs of honour and duels". It is placed in Cuba and Sucre street. The almost magic atmosphere which involves the well known "Casa del Angel" (Angel House) inspired the book of an Argentine writer, lately being represented in a film.

In front of the most antique Belgrano Plaza, in the corner of Cuba and Juramento, the historic Sarmiento Museum, exhibitis thirteen rooms with elements belonging to the life and work of this distinguished teacher, native of San Juan. There is a yard at the back where a sprout of a paraguayan lapacho exists, at the shadow of which Sarmiento "embroidered" his last remembrances.

*Museum (Old house) Yrurtia*

The Spanish art represented by a valuable collection of pictures, furniture and religious objects is one of the highest exponents of the colonial architecture. The Spanish Art Museum Enrique Larreta, bestowed by this outstanding writer is placed in Juramento 2291.

"Inmaculada Concepción" church which due to its curious structure is generally called "the Round", is the most traditional catholic church of Belgrano.

The outstanding sculptor Rogelio Yrurtia, transformed with his exquisite design in a Spanish baroque style, an old house of the XIX century; he was given the municipal prize in 1921 because of this work. Lately transferred to the State, it is set in O'Higgins 2390 as a museum, which keeps this splendid work.

Cabildo avenue, where the commercial galleries, restaurants, beer-saloons, tempt the passer-by, shows itself rich when it reaches Juramento avenue, typic corner of the quarter. Its colourful shop windows are always ready to receive the influence of fashion and seem to continue on the people walking around. Its development makes one imagine a generous future.


## General Paz Avenue

The wonderful asphaltic "waist" of selected trees, is decorated with multicolor flowers of the peculiar "casitas de los jardineros" (Gardeners Petty houses) which are placed all along its way. It is crossed by important routes and railway lines which join the capital with the neighbouring towns of Gran Buenos Aires. It is a quick hich speed comfortable way of communication.

Going south, it has its first intersection with Libertador Avenue, which leads to the Delta area. Keeping the same direction a little bit further, it is found the "acceso Norte" —Panamerican Route— which is the most easy way to important near-by towns.

The agreeable "Barrio Saavedra" (Saavedra quarter) where the historical museum Saavedra is set, is a remarkable ride due to the natural, architectonic and cultural attractions it possesses. The manorial house, during the last century property of Saavedra

*Saavedra Historical Museum – A deed from the past*

family, exhibits art works, and antiques of high value, being the most important the embroidered side combs, ellegant adorn for the ladies of the colonial society.

A few kilometres later, both Domingo Faustino Sarmiento railway line and long Rivadavia avenue, point out the populous Liniers quarter. Traditional San Cayetano Church, is visited on the seventh day of every month and specially on the 7th of August, by a great number of parishioners who venerate the image of the saint.

On passing Liniers and at the intersection with route N° 3 the typic "Mataderos" quarter is found. It is the concentration spot of the big "frigoríficos" (cold storage houses for meat), which surround the municipal Butchery. On the old Corrales avenue, which reminds the old carts which carried cattle, the Corrales "criollo" Museum has its site.

Going a little further, the magnificient highway General Richieri crosses it, and it leads to the International Ezeiza airport, going through wide woods with poly-sport stadiums.

At the end of this avenue it is found the Municipal autodrome, whit shining tracks, attracting fans of this sport. To associate the image of Juan Manuel Fangio to it, five times world motoring champion, is a constant and logic pride for Argentine people.

The huge portico of colonial style under the name of "Puente de la Noria" points out the ending line of this avenue, on the Riachuelo banks.


## SHOPPING

One of the most pleasant touristic motives is to walk, to watch at the shop windows, buying different articles, if they attract your attention. Actually Buenos Aires offers an infinite range of products, a true temptation for the visitor.

First rate articles which could be acquired at reasonable prices are possible to be found here.

One of the aims of this pocket guide is to help you saving time while searching and selecting commercial centers, where to buy the most important articles made in Argentina.

Only suggestions are listed as follows, within areas comprissing streets mentioned on each subject:


**Leather articles:**
Suipacha street, Florida street, Santa Fe avenue, Corrientes avenue.

**Shoemakers:**
Florida street, Suipacha street, Cerrito street, Alvear avenue, Quintana avenue, Santa Fe avenue, Corrientes avenue.

**Woollen articles:**
Florida street, Callao avenue, Santa Fe avenue, Corrientes avenue.

**Women, men and children clothes:**
Florida street, Esmeralda street, Carlos Pellegrini street, Santa Fe avenue, Corrientes avenue.

**Haute couture:**
Florida street, Maipú street, Rodríguez Peña street, Arroyo street, Quintana avenue, Alvear avenue, Arenales street, Santa Fe avenue.

**Cosmetics:**
Florida street, Esmeralda street, Suipacha street, Carlos Pellegrini street, Callao avenue, Corrientes avenue, Córdoba street, Santa Fe avenue, Quintana avenue, Alvear avenue.

**Furs:**
Florida street, Maipú street, Esmeralda street, Suipacha street, Cerrito street, Corrientes avenue, Tucumán street, Viamonte street, Córdoba avenue, Paraguay street, M. T. de Alvear street, Santa Fe avenue, Arenales street.

**Saddlery:**
Leandro N. Alem avenue, 25 de Mayo street, Reconquista street, Montes de Oca avenue, Constitución street, Directorio avenue, Díaz Vélez avenue, Santa Fe avenue.

**Jewellery:**
Florida street, Carlos Pellegrini street, Libertad street, Corrientes avenue, Santa Fe avenue.

**Sporting articles:**
Florida street, Esmeralda street, Maipú street, Suipacha street, Lima street, Cangallo street, Córdoba avenue, Santa FeFe avenue.

**Folk articles:**
25 de Mayo street, Reconquista street, San Martín street, Florida street, Maipú street, Esmeralda street, Suipacha street,

Callao avenue, Corrientes avenue, Tucumán street, Viamonte street, Córdoba avenue.

**Art masterpieces:**

San Martín street, Florida street, Suipacha street, Viamonte street, Córdoba avenue, Paraguay street, Santa Fe avenue, Defensa street.

**Antiquities:**

Libertador avenue, Defensa street, Montevideo street, Rodríguez Peña street, Libertad street, Callao avenue, M. T. de Alvear street, Quintana avenue, Arroyo street, Juncal street, Posadas street, Florida street.

*San Telmo Fair*

**Books, records and posters:**
Florida street, Maipú street, Suipacha street, May avenue, Callao Avenue, Sarmiento street, Corrientes avenue, Santa Fe avenue.

**Industrial machinery and tools:**
Perú street, Bolívar street, Chacabuco street, Belgrano avenue, Venezuela street, Moreno street.

**House ware articles:**
Florida street, Callao avenue, Pueyrredón avenue, Rivadavia avenue, Corrientes avenue, Córdoba avenue, Santa Fe avenue.

**Drinks:**
Reconquista street, San Martín street, Florida street, Cangallo street, Sarmiento street, Corrientes avenue, Córdoba avenue, Santa Fe avenue.

**Cloth and silk shops:**
Suipacha street, Lima street, Cabildo avenue, Santa Fe avenue, Corrientes avenue, Rivadavia avenue.

**Optics:**
Florida street, Esmeralda street, Suipacha street, Mayo avenue, Rivadavia avenue, Santa Fe avenue.

**Toy shops:**
Florida street, Maipú street, Avenida de Mayo, Rivadavia avenue, Sarmiento street, Corrientes avenue, Paraguay street, Santa Fe avenue, Cabildo avenue.

# EXCURSIONS FROM BUENOS AIRES
## Within your easy reach. . .

Besides Buenos Aires touristic attractions, we must refer to the neighouring localities. They own innumerable possibilities, not far from downtown area but with a "gift": the chance to change a simple excursion into a full knowledge of the historical and recreational sites. One point worth watching: our way of living. Now let's be off. . .

## San Antonio de Areco

This small locality situated 115 km towards northwest, connected with the capital via national route N° 8 and General Bartolomé Mitre Railway, has reguarlarly fixed timetable trips either by train or by bus. Actually this old prosperous city is proud to be one of the primitive villages that grew in Argentina pampa in the past, like the setting up of boundary marks to stop the sudden attack of indians.

The "Día de la Tradición" (day of tradition) is celebrated in November; then the gaucho's legacy is shown with splendor.

Many attractions are here, such as "Parque criollo" and "Museo Gauchesco Ricardo Güiraldes" (museum) on the bank of Areco river. Elements of costumes, weapons and other circumstances related to the customs and habits of the man of our land are shown. Pictorial works are also important because they keep some of famous fine art painters, such as Eduardo Sívori and Pedro Figari. The "pulpería La Blanqueada" (old retail grocery) shows a typical "boliche" (pub) belonging to the colonial epoch, with waxed shaped characters, reflecting the feelings and attitudes of countrymen.

San Antonio de Areco has recreational complements, the river, the bathing resort, the "Puente Viejo" (one of the oldest bridges of the country, and a unit of pleasant entertainments). It is the birth place of Ricardo Güiraldes, who had written one of the most important masterpieces of gauchesca literature: "Don Segundo Sombra" (pertaining the life of gauchos).

## Luján

Luján has a deep historical, religious and recreational root, only 64 km from downtown area; linked to the capital by means of national route N° 7 and Domingo Faustino Sarmiento railway, both with excellent regularly scheduled trips.

A fine museum unit called "Enrique Udaondo" attracts the attention of thousands of visitors week after week. High valued pieces of the colonial period are shown inside its sixty exhibition rooms.

Next to it the "Museo del Transporte" (museum of transportation means), where a variety of vehicles of different and old epoch are exhibited. There we may see the first tramways, the first locomotive engine, the first hydroplane, which had crossed the Atlantic ocean from Spain to Buenos Aires; varied models of carts, and an uncountable number of transportation means that changed the capitl long ago.

The "Basílica" of gothic style, with two towers, higher than 100 meters, congregates thousands of parishioners and pilgrims during the weekends. It is one of the most workshipped sanctuaries of our land. One site of privilege for those enthusiastic on outside activities is the bank of Río Luján, at the same time completed with an attractive recreational and gastronomic infrastructure.

## La Plata

Capital city of Buenos Aires province founded in 1882, by Dr. Dardo Rocha, it is an example of urbanistic creativity. This town is 56 km far from Buenos Aires, towards south. You reach

La Plata by means of the overlaying of national routes N° 1 and 2, or by General Roca railway, or excellent bus lines, at regular timetables.

A kind of competition, because of their pure architectonic lines, is played by its buildings: the Cathedral, of gothic lines, designed by engineer Pedro Benoit; the Law Courts, the town hall, the Government House, the "Teatro Argentino de La Plata" (theatre), etc.

The "Museo de Ciencias Naturales" (Natural Sciences museum) is situated near the wood. It is well known because of its paleontological collections.

Not far from La Plata is located a kind of urban entity called "República de los Niños": recreational building of a small scale copy of a city, with the annex of bordering woods and possibilities for camping fans.

The "Estación de Cría de Animales Salvajes" (breeding place for wild animals) with a rich variety of native and foreign fauna is situated in the center of "Parque Pereyra Iraola" (park).


## Chascomús

On the river bank of the Chascomús lagoon, about 132 km from the federal capital, it is one of the most popular towns of the southern part of the province. How to get there: by route N° 2, by General Roca railway, or by regular bus lines. It is of special attraction for fishemen and walkers by.

This lagoon, with an excellent fishing, keeps the attention of tourists, a fame acquired during years, because it offers wonderful varieties of mackerels, piece of special taste. But as an alternative, all chances for nautics are given by a group of clubs.

The "Parque los Libres del Sur" wood of 20 hectares, keeps inside the pampeano museum, designed in accordance with old regulations of colonial style. It seems to be a ressemblance of ancient post-houses and "mensajerías". Elements of native origin, the gaucho and his history, are exhibited all along its comfortable rooms.

The "Estación Hidrobiológica" (fish hatchery) where millions of pejerrey eggs are hatched annually, with the aim of keeping and improving the specie, is located in front of the museum. The laboratory with its procreation process, may be visited.

In Boulevard Lamadrid and Venezuela corner, is situated the "capilla de los Negros" (black people chapel). This singular and primitive church (1816) belongs to "Hermandad de los Morenos". No mass is given there, but the heir of old owners, maintains its tidiness, and affords the visitor entrance. This chapel, devoted to "La Virgen Morena de los Milagros", with a humble altar, brick walls at sight and an earth floor, has a great simplicity.

Chascomús has big campings, moren than twenty hotels and a good gastronomic infrastructure.

## Tigre and Delta

About half a hour from downtown area this zone is a frequented and splendid center. From the wharf of Tigre riverside station, a service of "lancha-colectivos" (bus motor boats) depart at fixed timetables; thus a fantastic trip may be taken in the midst of rivers and brooks, bordered by nice islands of an exceptional forest. Attractive residences and clubs for nautic activities, give a peculiar characteristic to the Delta.

Many crafts, small ships, lighters, and cargo vessels, move along the rivers and internal branch streams. Fishermen are pleased with greedy pieces like: gilthead, surubí, etc. No doubt natural beauty will captivate all tourists.

# BRIEF DESCRIPTION: THE MOST RELEVANT TOURISTIC CENTERS OF THE REPUBLIC

## Mar del Plata

Within the limits of Buenos Aires province, towards south, 404 km far from the federal capital, the city of Mar del Plata appears. Its was founded by Patricio Peralta Ramos in 1874. It is the principal southern summer resort of the Atlantic ocean, because of its beaches, buildings, variety of activities, and a special swing. A good touristic infrastructure, more than 1500 hotels, excellent gastronomic services, and may others, attract people to it. To go once means to go back.

How to get there: by national route Nº 2, bus lines, with fixed timetables during day and night; b y General Roca railway, by plane, with daily flights all year round. Flight time: 1 hour and 10 minutes.

## Cataratas del Iguazú

Situated in the northern part of the province of Misiones, it is a shared site with Paraguay and Brasil. Splendid waterfalls are surrounded by a huge forest, and were discovered by Spanish conqueror Alvar Núñez Cabeza de Vaca, in the XVI century.

By national route Nº 12, bus lines, and by plane, it is possible to arrive at this place. Flight time: 2 hours 10 minutes.

## Noroeste argentino

It covers the provinces of Jujuy, Salta, Tucumán, Catamarca, and La Rioja. Before the Spanish conquerors it was known as "camino del Inca" (Inca route) because people coming from Perú and Alto Perú entered our land by the famous Humahuaca Ravine. History as well as natural beauty are joined there.

How to get there: by route Nº 9, bus lines, by railway, with daily fixed timetables. By plane, but to the different airports of its principal capital cities; they may be reached in about 2 hours and 30 minutes flight.

## Región de Cuyo

Before the incomparable frame of Andean beauty, there appear the provinces of Mendoza, San Juan and San Luis, in an endless line of wine yards embellishing the fields, famous in the world wine-industry.

72

The high peaks of the Cordillera de los Andes, with eternal snowy mountains and fertile valleys; big ski courts and winter sports, spread tourism year after year.

How to get to this zone: by national route N°7, by General San Martín railway, bus lines and by plane, to the different airports comprising these provinces. Flight time: about 1 hour and 30 minutes.

## Bariloche

This first rate world known recreational touristic destination, of an imposing beauty, is an obligatory resort for skiers, beauty lovers and fishermen.

The lakes, woods, mountains, and a variety of motivations, frame a gate towards the dazzling world of snow and winter sports.

How to get there: excellent bus lines services, by General Roca railway, and by plane. Time of arrival: 2 hours 30 minutes.

## Córdoba

This province is a pioneer of tourism in Argentina. Its natural beauty, an excellent climate and a historical tradition grant a special tour. Within its limits a lot of touristic resorts, live and work day after day.

Hotels, gastronomic possibilities and extense provincial routes must be taken into account. Hundreds of centennial villages are inter-connected by routes.

How to get there: by national route N°8 and 9, bus services, by General Bartolomé Mitre Railway, and by plane —daily flights. Time of arrival: about 1 hour 10 minutes.

## Antártida

This paradise of snowy loneliness, silent and proud, full of paramount new landscapes, is at the same time, the place for many naval stations of the army forces.

In the midst of this splendid view a rich fauna —seals, marine elephants fur— bearing seals, a variety of water birds, and whales —give their living sound, a typical aspect of our polar region.

All along summer time many cruisers —tourists of the whole world— arrive at this destination, allowing them a wonderful tour, an unsurpassed beauty gift and the chance to visit its important scientific stations.

## Tierra del Fuego

This city situated in the southern part of the continent is the capital of the Territory. Groups of tourists arrive at its lodges to enjoy nature. How to get there: by national route N° 3 —3200 km from Buenos Aires; by sea: different navigation companies offer crusiers, specially when summer comes. During the whole year commercial ships arrive once a month. By plane airlines combine their flights with LADE. Time or arrival: 5 hours 30 minutes.

## Glaciar Perito Moreno

One of the most splendid phenomena is found in the southern limit of the continental part. This glacier, with a front part of 3 meters length and more than 50 meters width, year after year pushes forward from the Cordillera up to "Lago Argentino" originating a natural paramount scenery. From Santa Cruz province, by the provincial route or by airlines, it is possible to get to this place.

## Other important resorts

Although they are not mentioned here, many other destinations may be visited in the country. Lack of space has been our fault, if any.

# OUR GOOD-BYE

It is this the purpose of this pocket guide is you have a complete wiew of the peculiarities of Buenos Aires.

This city has as a characteristic: four fixed seasons, offering in such a way the visitor a possibility to enjoy it, at any time of the year. Average temperatures are as follows: summer time, 22.7 G.C., Autumn 14.4 G.C., Winter 12.2 G.C. and in Spring 19.9 G.C.

Traditionally speaking the "porteño" enjoys the meals. This way of living has conditioned the following timetables: Breakfast, from about 7.30 a.m. up to 8.30 a.m., generally composed by

*Restaurant in Buenos Aires*

coffee and milk, delicious "media lunas" (pastries), butter, "dulce de leche" (a kind of Argentine special milk marmalade) and jam. Lunch es taken from about 12 a.m. up to 2 p.m., usually includes two hot meals, fruit or dessert and coffee. Around 5 or 6 p.m. it is the habit to have a quick coffee or tea with some biscuits. At night, after daily work, the family gathers to dine from about 8 p.m. up to 10 p.m. Of course, this description is not a fixed pattern allowing ample changes due to working schedules or personal tastes.

Most of porteño typical meals are specialties of Argentina provinces, incorporated from many years for to the menu, because of its exquisite flavor. A hot small pie, full of meat or

*Invitation — Typical and international food*

vegetables is called "empanada". Famous barbecue and mixed grill, in the past, basic element belonging to "gaucho" food, are highly appreciated because Argentine meat is well known all round the world.

Our wealthy soil had afforded tthe vineyards to give exceptionally high quality wines that will satisfy all tastes. It is an Argentine habit to have wine during meals.

Among well known desserts of "criollo" (native) cuisine there are: "dulce de leche", sweet potato, calabash and popular "alfajores" (Sweet pies) with different tastes and forms, according to the zone of the country it comes from.

Certainly one of your souvenirs will be a "mate and bombilla" a reminder from Buenos Aires. This sweet and warm infusion, of a peculiar flavor is a healthy stimulant rich in mineral salts and vitamins. This beverage, inside a vessel, with bombilla (a metal tube with a mouthpiece at one end and a strainer at the other) is sucked up, passes from hand to hand, and links people together in a cordial way.

Friends meet to have "mate" together; this custom is a part of our living; you are kindly invited to share it.

Although the tango is the main musical gift, folk music and songs represent the landscapes and spirit of provincial people. Amidst lots of artists who had interpreted it we may mention: Atahualpa Yupanqui, Eduardo Falú, "Cuchi" Leguizamón, Mercedes Sosa, Jaime Torres, Ariel Ramírez, etc. A great number of excellent musical "conjuntos" (groups) had spread all over the world Argentine folklore.

The "poncho" of vicuña, alpaca, llama and sheep wool, done by female hands in homemade looms, was the fellow companion of our "gaucho". Nowadays different wool colours and drawings remind the regions where they come from. Its soft texture will keep you warm in cold days.

Our last words, this pocket guide goes with you, please let it return to our country inside one of your friends' pocket. Good luck, until next time.

CHAU, our affective way of saying:

GOOD BYE

# HOTELS

| | |
|---|---|
| Alvear Pace Hotel - Avda. Alvear 1891 | 41-4031 |
| Buenos Aires Sheraton Hotel - San Martín 1225 | 31-6310 |
| Carson Hotel - Viamonte 650 | 392-3551 |
| Castelar Hotel - Avda. de Mayo 1152 | 37-5001 |
| City Hotel - Bolivar 160 | 34-6481 |
| Claridge Hotel - Tucumán 535 | 32-3631 |
| Columbia Palace Hotel - Avda. Corrientes 1533 | 49-1993 |
| Continental - Avda. Pte. Roque Saenz Peña 725 | 46-4011 |
| Cosmos Hotel - Lima 1801 | 26-8282 |
| Crillón Hotel - Avda. Santa Fe 796 | 32-8181 |
| De la Paix - Rivadavia 1155 | 38-8061 |
| Diplomat Hotel - San Martín 918 | 32-5468 |
| Eldorado Hotel - Avda. Córdoba 622 | 392-1188 |
| Embajador Hotel - C. Pellegrini 1181 | 42-9644 |
| Español - Avda. de Mayo 1212 | 38-2091 |
| Fides Palace Hotel - Pavón 1281 | 26-5037 |
| Gran Hotel Argentino - C. Pellegrini 37 | 35-3071 |
| Gran Hotel Atlantic - Castelli 45 | 47-0081 |
| Gran Hotel Buenos Aires - Marcelo T. de Alvear 767 | 32-3031 |
| Gran Hotel Dorá - Maipú 963 | 32-7391 |
| Gran Hotel Eibar - Florida 328 | 45-7315 |
| Gran Hotel Orly - Paraguay 474 | 32-5344 |
| Gran Hotel Royal - Lavalle 570 | 31-4961 |
| Gran Hotel San Carlos - Suipacha 39 | 40-7021 |
| Impala - Libertad 1215 | 42-5107 |
| Italia Hotel Romanelli - Reconquista 645 | 32-6361 |
| Jousten Hotel - Avda. Corrientes 280 | 31-9591 |
| Jockey Club Hotel - Florida 568 | 392-8293 |
| King's Hotel - Avda. Corrientes 623 | 392-8161 |
| Lafayette Hotel - Reconquista 546 | 31-3021 |
| Liberty Hotel - Avda. Corrientes 626 | 46-0261 |
| Lincoln Hotel - San José 1299 | 27-4684 |
| Lyon - Riobamba 251 | 45-0101 |
| Madrid - Avda. de Mayo 1137 | 38-9021 |
| Monumental - Junin 357 | 49-8471 |
| Mundial - Avda. de Mayo 1298 | 37-0011 |
| Napoleón - Avda. Rivadavia 1364 | 37-2031 |
| Nogaró - Avda. Pte. Julio A. Roca 562 | 33-0091 |
| Normadie Hotel - Rodríguez Peña 320 | 40-7001 |
| Parlamento - Rodriguez Peña 61 | 46-1816 |
| Planeta - Paraguay 1420 | 41-2285 |
| Plaza Hotel - Florida 1005 | 31-5011 |
| Plaza Francia Hotel - E. Schiaffino 2189 | 42-9631 |

| | |
|---|---|
| Presidente - Cerrito 850 | 49-7671 |
| Promenade Hotel - Marcelo T. de Alvear 444 | 32-5681 |
| Regidor - Tucumán 451 | 32-9461 |
| Regis Hotel - Lavalle 813 | 392-5131 |
| República - Cerrito 370 | 35-5020 |
| Ritz - Avda. de Mayo 1111 | 37-9001 |
| Rivotel Esmeralda 540 | 392-0415 |
| Rochester Hotel - Esmeralda 542 | 392-5995 |
| Salles Hotel - Cerrito 208 | 35-0091 |
| San Antonio - Paraguay 372 | 32-5381 |
| Sarmiento Palace Hotel - Sarmiento 1953 | 45-3401 |
| Savoy Hotel - Avda. Callao 181 | 40-0151 |
| Sheltown - Marcelo T. de Alvear 742 | 32-5070 |
| Transocean - Lavalle 538 | 49-3241 |
| Tucumán Palace Hotel - Tucumán 384 | 31-3555 |
| Tres Sargentos - Tres Sargentos 345 | 32-6081 |
| Victory Hotel - Maipú 880 | 392-8415 |
| Waldorf - Paraguay 450 | 32-2070 |
| Washington Hotel - Suipacha 854 | 32-8426 |
| Wilton Palace Hotel - Avda. Callao 1162 | 41-1818 |

## RESTAURANTS

| | |
|---|---|
| ABC - Lavalle 545 | 31-3292 |
| Alfonso - Suipacha 545 | 392-6624 |
| Automóvil Club Argentino Avda. del Libertador 1850 | 80-1744 |
| Arturito - Corrientes 1124 | 35-0227 |
| Au Bec Fin - Arenales 1223 | 41-1144 |
| Au Coin de Marseille - Defensa 714 | 30-2324 |
| Bachin - Sarmiento 1617 | 46-7159 |
| Claridge - Tucumán 535 | 32-4001 |
| Claudio - Sarmiento 1550 | 35-5551 |
| Corrientes 11 - Avenida Corrientes 135 | 31-3895 |
| Chez Luis - Av. J. A. Roca 562 | 33-0091 |
| Chiquin - Cangallo 920 | 35-1966 |
| Don Juan - R. M. Ortiz 1827 | 41-5044 |
| Don Sancho - Suipacha 453 | 392-2854 |
| Drugstore - R. M. Ortiz 1747 | 44-8477 |
| El Aljibe - San Martín 1225 | 31-6310 |
| El Caldero - Gorriti 3972 | 89-2335 |

| | |
|---|---|
| El Ceibal - Av. Callao 1056 | 41-6711 |
| El Ceibal - Güemes 3402 | 84-5807 |
| El Ciervo - Callao 392 | 45-3391 |
| El Emporio de la Papa Frita - Maipú 431 | 392-2800 |
| El Fogón de Martín Fierro - Av. Pte. Fig. Alcorta | 782-7204 |
| El Globo - Hip. Yrigoyen 1199 | 38-3926 |
| El Gran Puchero - Medrano 1071 | 86-2220 |
| El Imparcial - Hip. Yrigoyen 1201 | 37-2919 |
| El Imperio de la Papa Soufle- Maipú 558 | 392-4563 |
| El Mirasol - Boedo 136 | 89-5890 |
| El Nacional de San Telmo - Bolívar 315 | 34-9614 |
| El Palacio de la Papa Frita - Lavalle 735 | 392-5844 |
| El Palacio de la Papa Frta - Lavalle 954 | 392-1599 |
| El Palacio de la Papa Frita Av. Corrientes 1612 | 46-8063 |
| El Rancho de Ochoa - Catamarca 999 | 97-2724 |
| El Recodo - Lavalle 130 ) | 32-2453 |
| El Repecho de San Telmo - C. Calvo 242 | 34-4473 |
| El Rey del Bife - Paraná 378 | 46-8568 |
| El Toboso - Corrientes 1838 | 45-0519 |
| El Tropezón - Av. Callao 248 | 45-6453 |
| French Can-Can - Eduardo Acevedo 71 | 90-5333 |
| Giorgio - Talcahuano 1123 | 41-7074 |
| Grill Santa Generosa - Florida 570 | 392-2185 |
| Harrod's Florida 877 | 32-4411 |
| Hispano - Salta 26 | 38-5325 |
| Hostería del Caballito Blanco - M. T. de Alvear 479 | 31-1889 |
| Il Pozzo de Poeta - Avda. del Libertador 6649 | 782-6880 |
| Jai Lai - Juramento 2790 | 783-2493 |
| José Av. Cabildo 1741 | 73-6418 |
| Joxe Txiki (Restaurante vasco) - Belgrano 1211 | 37-1559 |
| Kalispera - Montevideo 779 | |
| King George II - Santa Fé 2835 | 84-1626 |
| La Banderita - San Juan 3268 | 93-3580 |
| La Belle Epoque - Arribeños 3668 | 701-4851 |
| La Biela - R. M. Ortiz 1887 | 42-0449 |
| La Cabaña - Av. Entre Ríos 436 | 38-2373 |
| La Cantina China - Maipú 967 | 32-7391 |
| La Carreta - Av. del Libertador 6902 | 782-8968 |
| La Casona de Roque - Inclán 2558 | 941-2063 |
| La Central - Lavalle y Esmeralda | 392-4261 |
| La Emiliana - Corrientes 1443 | 40-5704 |
| La Estancia - Lavalle 941 | 35-0336 |
| Lagar del Virrey - Ayacucho 1169 | 44-2956 |
| La Tablita - Maipú 548 | 392-5500 |
| La Tranquera - Av. Pte. Fig. Alcorta 6466 | 73-6119 |
| La Rastra - Salguero 1133 | 86-6901 |

| | |
|---|---|
| La Raya - Pavón 3062 | 941-5782 |
| La Veda - Florida 1 | 33-8680 |
| La Veda de San Telmo - Cochabamba 267 | 34-4034 |
| Lo Prete - L. Saenz Peña 749 | 38-7393 |
| Mamma Leone - Sacalabríni Ortiz 3624 | 71-7169 |
| Mesón Español - Av. Caseros 1750 | 26-6885 |
| Michelangelo - Balcarce 433 | 33-5392 |
| Mikado - Conesa 898 | 781-4254 |
| Monty's - Honduras 3760 | 87-5127 |
| Munich Corrientes - Av. Corrientes 1220 | 35-1354 |
| Munich Esmeralda - Esmeralda 444 | 392-7427 |
| Otto - Berutti 3270 | 83-4624 |
| Pampa Grill - San Martín 1225 | 31-6310 |
| Pipo S.R.L. - Montevideo 341 | 46-0762 |
| Restaurant Pedemonte - Esmeralda 59 | 33-3641 |
| Rocinante - C. Pellegrini 713 | 392-1992 |
| Sorrento - Avda. Corrientes 668 | 45-3787 |
| Tavola Calda Luiggi - Anchorena 883 | 88-5515 |
| The London Grill - Reconquista 455 | 31-2223 |
| Tomo I - B. G. J. M. de Rosas 1598 | 783-7479 |
| Veracruz - Uruguay 538 | 40-1413 |

## CANTINAS

| | |
|---|---|
| Baticueva - Necochea 1396 | 21-0440 |
| Cantina Cirigiliano - Anchorena 664 | 88-4347 |
| Capitán Tito - P. de Mendoza 2117 | |
| Casa del Atún - Almte. Brown 1227 | 28-4080 |
| Di Notte - Anchorena 924 | 85-0658 |
| Don Carlos - Billinghurst 450 | 86-9922 |
| Don Carlos II - Lavalle 771 | |
| El Dorado - P. de Mendoza 1455 | 21-3157 |
| El Pescadito - P. De Mendoza 1483 | 21-1640 |
| El Tiburón - P. de Mendoza 1561 | 21-3568 |
| Fechoría - Uruguay 74 | 38-5562 |
| I Giovanotti - Av. Corrientes 3469 | 86-1889 |
| Il Piccolo Navío - Necochea 1198 | 21-4055 |
| Il Vero Mangiare - Guardia Vieja 3470 | 86-4227 |
| Il Vero Fechoría - Córdoba 3915 | 88-4342 |
| La Barca de Bachicha - P. De Mendoza 1619 | |
| La Barca de Noé - Angel Gallardo 543 | 55-0886 |
| La Cueva de Zingarella - Necochea esq. Olavarría | 21-0736 |
| La Gaviota - Necochea 1254 | 28-4378 |

Los Troncos - Necochea 1265
Nicolita - Lamadrid y del V. Iberlucea
Norte - M. T. de Alvear 786                              32-8778
Praiano - Suarez 301                                     21-8463
Rímini - Necochea 1234
Spadavecchia - Necochea 1180                             21-4977
Tres Amigos - Necochea esq. Suarez

## CINEMAS

| | |
|---|---:|
| ABC - Esmeralda 506 | 392-9506 |
| Adan - Av. Corrientes 959 | 392-6115 |
| Alfa - Lavalle 842 | 392-1114 |
| Alfil - Corrientes 1753 | 40-7575 |
| Ambassador - Lavalle 777 | 392-9700 |
| América - Av. Callao 1057 | 41-3818 |
| Arizona - Lavalle 727 | 392-9667 |
| Arte - Diagonal Norte 1156 | 35-7934 |
| Ateneo - Paraguay 918 | 31-2888 |
| Atlas - Lavalle 869 | 392-1936 |
| Auditorio Kraft - Florida 683 | 392-2775 |
| Avenida - Av. de Mayo 675 | 33-6626 |
| Beta - Lavalle 925 | 35-1850 |
| Biarritz - Suipacha 482 | 392-0356 |
| Broadway - Av. Corrientes 1155 | 35-2345 |
| Callao - Callao 27 | 40-1898 |
| Capitol - Santa Fe 1848 | 44-2379 |
| Cinema I - Suipacha 460 | 392-1112 |
| Cinemateca - Sarmiento 2255 | 48-2170 |
| Cosmos 70 - Av. Corrientes 2046 | 49-0862 |
| Electric - Lavalle 836 | 392-1846 |
| Gaumont - Av. Rivadavia 1635 | 40-3050 |
| Gloria - Avda. de Mayo 1225 | 38-6966 |
| Gran Rex - Av. Corrientes 857 | 392-8000 |
| Gran Splendid - Av. Santa Fe 1860 | 44-0808 |
| Ideal - Suipacha 378 | 35-3310 |
| Iguazú - Lavalle 940 | 392-4431 |
| Leopoldo Lugones - Corrientes 1530 | |
| Libertador - Corrientes 1334 | 40-7443 |
| Loire - Corrientes 1524 | 49-1900 |
| Lorange - Corrientes 1372 | 45-7386 |
| Lorca - Corrientes 1428 | 40-5017 |
| Lorena - Corrientes 1551 | 46-7501 |

| | |
|---|---|
| Lorraine - Corrientes 1524 | |
| Los Angeles - Corrientes 1770 | 40-3742 |
| Losuar - Corrientes 1743 | 40-6100 |
| Luxor - Lavalle 669 | 392-3893 |
| Metro - Cerrito 570 | 35-4219 |
| Metrópolitan - Corrientes 1343 | 40-0816 |
| Monumental - Lavalle 780 | 392-4815 |
| Normandie - Lavalle 861 | |
| Ocean - Lavalle 739 | 392-1515 |
| Opera - Corrientes 860 | 35-1335 |
| Paramount - Lavalle 845 | 392-9999 |
| París - Lavalle 769 | 392-2016 |
| Plaza - Corrientes 939 | 392-5717 |
| Premier - Corrientes 1565 | 46-2113 |
| Real - Esmeralda 425 | 392-3600 |
| Renacimiento - Lavalle 925 | |
| Royal - Corrientes 831 | 392-8509 |
| Santa Fe I - Santa Fe 1947 | |
| Santa Fe II - Santa Fe 1947 | |
| Sarmiento - Lavalle 852 | 392-3338 |
| Select Lavalle - Lavalle 921 | 35-0235 |
| Studio - Santa Fe 2541 | 821-5845 |
| Suipacha - Suipacha 442 | 392-1995 |
| Trocadero - Lavalle 820 | 392-1455 |

## THEATRES

## Teatro Colón (Colón Theatre) - Libertad 621 - Te. 35-1430

The first steps and project of this building had been under the direction of engineer Francisco Tamburini. Ten years later architect Víctor Meano and Julio Dormal finished it. In 1908 (May 25th) it was inaugurated by means of the performance of the Opera Aída (Giuseppe Verdi).

The external features provoke admiration because of the harmonic and balanced adjustment of the constituting elements, an inspiration of architectonic styles of several epochs.

Each one of its rooms with a rich internal ornamentation, condition the audience to be astonished by the beatiful central parlor. The velvet "platea", golden seats, imposing stage, the enormous lamp, all shine under the exquisite arch, a masterpiece of Argentine painter Raúl Soldi. The musical hierarchy of this national stable cast, is at the same level of the most famous international artist.

**Teatro Nacional Cervantes** (Cervantes Theatre) - Av. Córdoba y Libertad - 46-8881

Since September 1921 this is a friendly corner for all "porteños", with a peculiar Spanish style.

A splendid inner decoration ressembles the traces left by important stage performances of the different casts that had passed through it.

**Teatro Municipal General San Martín** - Av. Corrientes 1530 - Te. 40-0111

This complex for theatrical expressions covers three rooms, "Martín Coronado", "Juan A. Casacuberta" and "Leopoldo Lugones". The great hall for exhibitions "Carlos Morel", the modern art museum and the Fine Arts Museum "Eduardo Sívori" are constantly visited, due to the attractive samples of esthetic pieces. Lecture rooms, permanent site for congresses and seminars, and LS1 Radio Ciudad de Buenos Aires are found inside this building.

Organization of space, adapted for the functions of this environment, is a product of constant creativity of architect Mario R. Alvarez, thus impressing a kind of personal seal to each one of his plays.

# OTHER THEATRES

| | |
|---|---|
| Argentino - Bme. Mitre 1448 | 38-9712 |
| Armando Discépolo - Pichincha 53 | 48-0682 |
| Astral - Corrientes 1639 | 46-5707 |
| Astros - Corrientes 746 | 45-5541 |
| Ateneo - Paraguay 918 | 31-2888 |
| Avenida - Av. de Mayo 1222 | 38-2295 |
| Blanca Podestá - Corrientes 1283 | 35-2592 |
| Colíseo - M. T. Alvear 1125 | |
| Colonial - P. Colón y Belgrano | 34-7958 |
| Cómico - Corrientes 1280 | 35-2108 |
| Chacabuco - Chacabuco 947 | 27-0819 |
| De la Fábula - Agüero 444 | 87-4531 |
| De la Ribera - P. de Mendoza 1843 | 28-1536 |
| Del Globo - M. T. de Alvear 1155 | 41-8351 |
| Eckos - Rivadavia 2215 | 45-3869 |
| Embassy - Suipacha 751 | 392-4450 |
| Empire - H. Yrigoyen 1934 | 47-8770 |
| El Nacional - Corrientes 960 | 35-7800 |
| Estrellas - Riobamba 280 | 46-6759 |
| I.F.T. - Boulogne Sur Mer 547 | 88-9420 |
| Lasalle - Cangallo 2263 | 47-9388 |
| Liceo - Rivadavia 1495 | 38-4291 |
| Maipo - Esmeralda 443 | 392-4882 |
| Municipal Enrique S. Discépolo - Corrientes 1659 | 46-6076 |
| Municipal Presidente Alvear - Corrientes 1659 | 46-6076 |
| Odeón - Esmeralda 367 | 45-3635 |
| Payró - San Martín 766 | |
| Regina - Santa Fe 1235 | 44-5470 |
| Santa María - Montevideo 842 | 42-7311 |
| S. H. A. - Sarmiento 2255 | |

## CAFE-CONCERTS

Aristóbulo - Tres Sargentos 415
El Gallo Cojo - Defensa 718
El Papagayo - R. M. Ortíz 1674
Cabaret - M. T. de Alvear 628
La Cebolla - Bmé. Mitre 1758
La Ciudad - Talcahuano 1034
La Fusa - Santa Fe 1883
La Gallina Embarazada - Libertad 1069
La Potra Piano Bar - Reconquista 869
La Rueda Cuadrada - Defensa 740
Michelangelo - Balcarce 433

# TANGUERIAS

Bar Sur - Balcarce 896
Cambalache - Libertad 822
Caño 14 - Talcahuano 975
El Viejo Almacén - Independencia y Balcarce
La Tanguería de Don Emilio - Defensa 760
Malena al Sur - Balcarce 854
Michelangelo - Balcarce 433
Patio de Tango - Corrientes 1162
Tango Bar - Bolivar 315
Tanguería Sur - Belgrano 1178
Tanguería Uno - La Rioja y P. Echague
Unión Bar - Paseo Colón 807
Vieja Recova
Viejo Rincón

# MUSEUMS

Please phone for time tables and visiting days

| | |
|---|---|
| Argentino de Ciencias Naturales | |
| "Bernardino Rivadavia" - Av. Angel Gallardo 470 | 87-1154 |
| Botánico - Av. Las Heras 4102 | |
| Criollo de los Corrales - Av. de los Corrales 6476 | 60-2741 |
| de Aduanas - Azopardo 350 | 33-9892 |
| de Armas de la Nación - Av. Santa Fe 750 | 32-9774 |
| de Arte Casa de Rogelio Yrurtia - O'Higgins 2390 | 781-6155 |
| de Arte Lírico del Teatro Colón - A. Toscanini 1150 | 35-5414 |
| de Arte Moderno - Av. Corrientes 1530 | 49-4796 |
| de Artes Plásticas "Eduardo Sívori" - Av. Corrientes 1530 | 46-9664 |
| de Bellas Artes - Av. del Libertador 1473 | 83-8814 |
| de Bellas Artes de La Boca - P. de Mendoza 1835 | 21-1080 |
| de Calcos y Escultura Comparada | |
| "Ernesto de la Cárcova" | |
| Avda. Costanera Sur esq. Brasil | 32-3790 |
| de la Casa de Gobierno - H. Irigoyen 219 | 34-0421 |
| de la Ciudad - Alsina 412 | 40-0111 |
| De la Policía Federal - San Martín 353 | 45-6857 |
| del Instituto Nacional Sanmartiniano - Pza. Grand Bourg sobre | |
| Castilla y Aguado | 83-3311 |
| Del Traje - Chile 832 | 30-8427 |
| Etnográfico "Juan B. Ambrosetti" - Moreno 350 | 34-4970 |

Fragata "Presidente Sarmiento" - Dársena Norte alt. Viamonte
Histórico de la Ciudad de Buenos
Aires "Brig. Gral. C. Saavedra" - Republiquetas 6309       51-0746
Histórico Nacional - Defensa 1600       26-4588
Histórico Nacional del Cabildo - Bolivar 65       30-1782
Histórico Sarmiento - Cuba 2079       73-4600
Mitre - San Martín 336       49-2659
Municipal de Arte Español "Enrique
Larreta" - Juramento 2291       73-4040
Municipal de Arte Hispano Americano
"Isaac Fernandez Blanco" - Suipacha 1422       41-9349
Municipal de Motivos Populares
Argentinos "José Hernandez" - Av. del Libertador 2373       83-9967
Nacional de Aeronáutica - Av. R. Obligado 4550
Nacional de Arte Decorativo - Av. del Libertador 1902       83-0914
Nacional de Arte Oriental - Av. del Libertador 1902 1er. Piso.       80-3988
Planetario Municipal de la
Ciudad de Buenos Aires
"Galileo Galilei"
Av. Sarmiento y Av. Pte. Figueroa Alcorta       771-6629


## SPORTING STADIUMS

Autódromo Municipal de la Ciudad de Bs. As., - Avda. General Paz y Avda.
Cnel Roca
Campo Argentino de Pato - Av. del Libertador y Dorrego
Campo Municipal de Golf - Tornquist y Olleros
Circuito K. D. T. - Av. Pte. Fig. Alcorta y A. Sarmiento
Club Hípico Argentino - Av. Pte. Fig. Alcorta y Basavilbaso
Hipódromo de Palermo - Av. del Libertador y Dorrego
Palacio de los Deportes Estadio
"Luna Park" - Av. Corrientes y Buchardo
Tiro Federal Argentino - Av. del Libertador 6935
Velódromo Municipal - Parque 3 de Febrero


## FOOTBALL STADIUMS

All Boys - Jonte y Mercedes
Argentinos Juniors - Juan A. Garcia y Boyacá
Atlanta - Humboldt 408
Banfield - Peña y Arenales (Banfield)
Boca Juniors - Brandsen 805
Chacarita Juniors - Gutierrez 351 - V. Maipú (San Martín)

Estudiantes de la Plata - Calle 1 entre 54 y 57 (La Plata)
Ferrocarril Oeste - Martín de Gainza 250
Gimnasia y Esgrima de la Plata - Calle 60 y 118 (La Plata)
Huracán - Av. Amancio Alcorta y Luna
Independiente - Almte. Cordero 751 (Avellaneda)
Quilmes - Guid y Sarmiento (Quilmes)
Racing - Cuyo 250 (Avellaneda)
River Plate - Avda. Pte. Fig. Alcorta 7597
San Lorenzo - Avda. La Plata 1674
Temperley - 9 de julio 310 (Temperley)
Velez Sarsfield - Jonte y Reservistas Argentinos

## USEFUL INFORMATION

| | |
|---|---:|
| Jorge Newbery Airport - Avenida Costanera Rafael Obligado entre Av. Sarmiento y La Pampa | 773-2011 |
| Air Terminal Station - Bartolomé Mitre y Ecuador | 88-7081 |
| Ezeiza International Airport - Ezeiza - Prov. de Bs. As. | 620-0217 |
| Dirección Nacional de Turismo - Santa Fe 883 | 32-2232 |
| ENTEL - Empresa Nacional de Telecomunicaciones (Long distance and international calls) - Av. Corrientes 707 | 45-6956 |
| (Telefonogramas Telex) | 012-2310 |
| (Telefonogramas - Phone) | 33-9251 |
| Argentine Railways: | |
| Domingo F. Sarmiento - Bartolomé Mitre 2815 | 87-0041 |
| General Bartolomé Mitre - Av. Dr. Ramos Mejía 1302 | 32-6596 |
| General Manuel Belgrano - Av. Dr. Ramos Mejía 1430 | 31-5287 |
| General José de San Martín - Av. Dr. Ramos Mejía 1552 | 31-9217 |
| General Julio A. Roca - General Hornos 11 | 23-0021 |
| General Justo J. de Urquiza - Av. Lacroze y Av. Corrientes | 55-5214 |
| Central Post - Office - Leandro N. Alem 337 | 31-5031 |
| Children Hospital - Gallo 1330 | 86-6831 |
| Urgency Municipal Hospital - Av. de Mayo 525 | 34-4001 |
| Hospital Alvarez - | 61-6666 |
| Hospital Durand | 89-6087 |
| Hospital Rivadavia | 83-0011 |
| Central Police Headquarters - Moreno 1550 | 38-8041 |
| Federal Police - (Personal documents, passports) - Cevallos 362 | 37-3107 |

## CURRENCY

Official state currency of legal term is the peso Law 18188, issued in bank notes of 10.000, 1.000, 500, 100. Coins circulate in different values of: 10, 5 and 1.

Foreign tourists may exchange money in places authorized by the National Central Bank of the Republic, in full accordance with the fluctuation of the day.

## EXCHANGE AGENCIES

América - San Martín 312
Andrés Domingo - San Martín 529
Baires S.A. - San Martín 215
Baldino - Av. Corrientes 328
Baupesa - San Martín 363
Bellizi - Av. Rivadavia 1823 2do. B
Casa Piano S.A. - San Martín 347
Exprinter S.A. - San Martín 176
Hermes S.A. - San Martín 317
Intercam S.A. - San Martín 318
Mercurio - San Martín 229
Olimpic - Av. Córdoba 433
Puente Hnos. S.A. - Lavalle 445
Puente Hnos. S.A. - Sarmiento 399
Velox - San Martín 298

## BANKS

Alemán Transatlántico - Bme. Mitre 401
Argentino de Comercio - Sarmiento 454
Bank of América - Maipú 250
Caja Nacional de Ahorro y Seguro - Hipólito Yrigoyen 1750
Central de la República Argentina - San Martín 275
Comercial de Buenos Aires - Av. Corrientes 2516
Cooperativo Agrario Argentino - Av. Cordoba 1154
de Crédito Rural Argentino - Bme. Mitre 343
de Italia y Rio de la Plata - Bme. Mitre 402
de la Ciudad de Buenos Aires - Florida 302
de la Nación Argentina - Bme. Mitre 326
de la Provincia de Buenos Aires - San Martín 137
Del Interior y Buenos Aires - Cangallo 485
de Londres y América del Sud - Reconquista 101
de Santander - Bme. Mitre 575
di Napoli - Av. Pres. R. Saenz Peña 660
do Brasil S.A. - Cangallo 580

Español del Río de la Plata - Reconquista 200
Federal Argentino - Sarmiento 401
First National City Bank of New York - Bme. Mitre 502
Francés del Río de la Plata - Reconquista 199
del Sud - Cangallo 500
Holandés Unido - 25 de Mayo 81
Internacional - Sarmiento 532
Italo Belga - Cangallo 338
Nuevo Banco Italiano - Av. Rivadavia 401
Popular Argentino - Florida 201
Río de la Plata - Cangallo 541
Shaw'- Sarmiento 355
Superville de Buenos Aires Societé
Generale - Reconquista 330
The Bank of Tokyo Ltd. - Maipú 316
The First National Bank of Boston - Florida 99
The Royal Bank of Canada - Florida 202
Tornquist - Bme. Mitre 531s,


# AIRLINE COMPANIES

| | |
|---|---:|
| Aerolíneas Argentinas  Perú 22 | 30-8551 |
| Aerolíneas Colonia - Uruguay 467 8vo. A | 49-6403 |
| Aero Perú - Av. Santa Fe 840 | 31-4115 |
| Air France - Florida 894 | 32-7349 |
| Alia - Paraguay 729 | 32-4035 |
| Alitalia - Santa Fe 887 | 32-4086 |
| Austral - Av. R. S. Peña 737 | 46-8811 |
| Avianca - Av. Santa Fe 865 | 32-3693 |
| Braniff Internacional - Santa Fe 881 | 34-0031 |
| British Caledonian - Cordoba 650 | 392-7611 |
| Canadian Pacific - Cordoba 656 | 392-3765 |
| Cruzeiro - Cerrito 1026 | 41-1061 |
| Ecuatoriana - Tucumán 719 | 392-9697 |
| El Al - Maipú 464 | 392-7658 |
| Iberia - Av. R. Saenz Peña 947 | 35-2050 |
| Japan Air Lines - Cordoba 858 | 392-7198 |
| K L M - Florida 989 | 31-8921 |
| LADE - Perú 714 | 34-7071 |
| Lan-Chile - Cordoba 879 | 31-5334 |
| LAP - 25 de Mayo 575 | 31-0418 |
| Lloyd Aéreo Boliviano - Cordoba 303 | 32-1529 |
| Lufthansa - M.T. de Alvear 636 | 32-8171 |
| Pan American - Av. R. Saenz Peña 832 | 45-0111 |

| | |
|---|---|
| PLUNA - Lavalle 528 | 45-8210 |
| Sabena - Av. Santa Fe 816 | 31-3040 |
| SAS - Florida 902 | 32-8161 |
| South African Airways - Av. Santa Fe 790 | 31-8199 |
| Swissair - Av. Santa Fe 846 | 31-8930 |
| TAP - Av. Santa Fe 989 | 42-9811 |
| TWA - Cordoba 669 ero. | 31-9237 |
| Varig - Av. R. Saenz Peña 950 | 35-2017 |
| VIASA - Florida 989 | 31-8921 |

## NAVIGATION COMPANIES

| | |
|---|---|
| Alimar S.A. - M.T. de Alvear 1199 | 44-9551 |
| Cacciola - Av. Cazón 1581 - Tigre | 749-0931 |
| ELMA - Av. Corrientes 389 | 32-4861 |
| Flota Fluvial del Estado  Argentino - Av. Corrientes 389 | 31-0728 |
| Ferritur - Av. Corrientes 480 | 46-0103 |
| ONDA - Florida 502 | 3922-5011 |
| Blue Star Line - Cordoba 657 | 392-2471 |
| Italmar - Cordoba 629 | 392-5325 |
| Línea C - Florida 986 | 31-5241 |
| Royal Mail Line - 25 de Mayo 499 | 31-4761 |
| Ybarra - 25 de Mayo 464 | 31-4711 |

## FOREIGN REPRESENTATIVES

| | |
|---|---|
| GERMANY - Maipú 942 piso 18 | 32-9424 |
| Rep. ARABE UNIDA - Guido 1530 piso 1 "B" | 42-8542 |
| ALGERIA - Montevideo 1889 | 44-4969 |
| AUSTRALIA - Santa Fe 846 piso 7 | 32-6841 |
| AUSTRIA - French 3671 | 72-7095 |
| BELGIUM - Defensa 113 piso 8 | 33-0066 |
| BOLIVIA - 25 de Mayo 611 piso 2 | 31-7365 |
| BRAZIL - Paraguay 580 piso 2 | 31-7743 |
| BULGARIA - Manuel Obarrio 2967 | 83-7458 |
| CANADA - Suipacha 1111 piso 25 | 32-9081 |
| COLOMBIA - Santa Fe 782 piso 8 | 31-4381 |
| COREA DEL SUR - Figueroa Alcorta 3221 | 83-4633 |
| COSTA RICA - Av. del Libertador 1146 | 42-6181 |
| CZECHOSLOVAKIA - Figueroa Alcorta 3240 | 80-3917 |
| CHILE - San Martín 439 piso 9 | 49-8171 |
| CUBA - Virrey del Pino 1810 | 73-4349 |

| | | |
|---|---|---:|
| DENMARK - L. N. Alem 1074 piso 9 | | 32-6901 |
| REP. DOMINICANA - Maipú 844 | | 392-2381 |
| ECUADOR - Av. Quintana 585 piso 10 | | 42-6408 |
| SPAIN - Guido 1760 | | 41-0078 |
| UNITED STATES - Sarmiento 669 piso 3 | | 46-3211 |
| PHILIPPINES - Castex 3123 piso 2 | | 80-5068 |
| FINLAND - Santa Fe 846 piso 5 | | 32-0600 |
| FRANCE - Santa Fe 846 piso 4 | | 32-2425 |
| GREAT BRITAIN - Dr. Luis Agote 2412 | | 80-7070 |
| GREECE - Av. Pte. R. Saenz Peña 547 p. 4 | | 34-3948 |
| GUATEMALA - Lavalle 1759 piso 6 | | 46-4647 |
| HAITI - Viamonte 1167 piso 8 | | 45-8796 |
| HOLLAND - Maipú 66 piso 2 | | 34-8778 |
| HONDURAS - Rodríguez Peña 336 piso 2 | | 40-0484 |
| HUNGARY - Coronel Díaz 1874 | | 83-0767 |
| INDIA - Paraguay 580 piso 3 | | 31-3020 |
| INDONESIA - Mariscal R. Castilla 2901 | | 80-6622 |
| IRAN - Ocampo 2901 | | 83-9314 |
| IRELAND - Santa Fe 782 piso 7 | | 32-4360 |
| ICELAND - Av. J. A. Roca 610 piso 7 | | 30-3353 |
| ISRAEL - Arroyo 910 | | 392-4481 |
| ITALY - M. T. de Alvear 1149 | | 42-9841 |
| JAMAICA - Corrientes 127 piso 4 | | 31-4872 |
| JAPAN - Azcuénaga 1035 | | 83-1031 |
| LEBANON - Av. del Libertador 2354 | | 821-0466 |
| MEXICO - Córdoba 1367 piso 8 | | 42-0723 |
| NICARAGUA - Venezuela 1460 piso 2 | | 37-8375 |
| NORWAY - Esmeralda 909 piso 3 | | 32-1904 |
| PAKISTAN - Av. Alvear 1402 piso 5 | | 42-1040 |
| PANAMA - Talcahuano 1038 piso 5 | | 42-9651 |
| PARAGUAY - Maipú 464 piso 3 | | 392-6536 |
| PERU - Corrientes 330 piso 3 | | 31-3374 |
| POLAND - A. M. Aguado 2870 | | 821-9781 |
| PORTUGAL - Córdoba 315 piso 3 | | 32-3524 |
| RUMANIA - Arroyo 962 | | 392-2630 |
| EL SALVADOR - Talcahuano 1038 piso 2 | | 42-6192 |
| REP. DEM. ALEMANA - Olazábal 2201 | | 781-2002 |
| REP. POPULAR CHINA - Sucre 3001 | | 73-1950 |
| SYRIA - Callao 956 | | 41-0486 |
| SOUTH AFRICA - M. T. de Alvear 590 piso 8 | | 31-8991 |
| SWEDEN - Corrientes 330 piso 3 | | 31-3080 |
| SWITZERLAND - Santa Fe 846 piso 12 | | 31-6491 |
| THAILANDIA - Belgrano 265 piso 9 | | 33-3690 |
| TURKEY - Av. R. Saenz Peña 852 piso 8 | | 46-8779 |
| U.R.S.S. - Guido 1677 | | 42-3315 |
| URUGUAY - Corrientes 545 piso 6 | | 49-4129 |

VENEZUELA - Esmeralda 909 piso 4          31-8337
VIET-NAM - Córdoba 1184                   46-6533
YUGOSLAVIA - Rodriguez Peña 1012          41-1309
ZAIRE - Villanueva 1356 piso 2            771-0075

## TOURISM AGENCIES AND ENTERPRISES

AGENCIA NICOLAS PUENTE - Av. Corrientes 516
ASENCIO TOURS S.A. - Av. Córdoba 669
ASI TUR - Cerrito 1070
BAITUR S.A. - Sarmiento 559 4 piso
CALCOS S.R.L. - Suipacha 760
C.A.V.I. S.A. - Rodriguez Peña 1122
C.I.T. S.A. - Av. Córdoba 369
CLUB DE VACACIONES - Av. de Mayo 1375
DELFINO TURISMO - San Martín 427
DODERO VIAJES - Sarmiento 440
EVES S.A. - Tucumán 702
EXPRINTER S.A. - San Martín 176
FURLONG S.R.L. - Cangallo 460
HOLDITUR - Tucumán 834 1 piso
LONGUEIRA Y LONGUEIRA - Av. Belgrano 1824
MELIA - Tucumán 637 5 piso
MERCOGLIANO - Montevideo 93
MUNDUS - 25 de Mayo 574
ONDA ARGENTINA - Florida 502
PADOVANI S.A. - Santa Fe 1159
POLVANI - Maipú 848
TELETOUR - Cerrito 798
TOURING CLUB ARGENTINO - Esmeralda 601
VACACIONES S.R.L. - Florida 877
VELOX S.R.L. - San Martín 298
WAGON'S LITS COOK - Av. Córdoba 685
ZENIT VIAJES - Paraguay 434

There are lots of important agencies and enterprises, although they are not listed here but anyway you can reach them, where you will be offered excellent services and amicable help. Look for them.

## Guides

If you want to ensure you are shown around Buenos Aires by an experienced well —informed person, choose one of the officially registered guides, because they have received special training.

**CONTENTS**

SE TERMINO DE IMPRIMIR EN LOS TALLERES
GRAFICOS DIJI S.R.L. SALCEDO 3442 - CAPITAL.
EN EL MES DE MAYO DE 1978.